To: Rhisa!

# GOD IS DOING
## A NEW THING...
# BECOMING
## A NEW PEOPLE!

May God bless and
refresh you!

Althea T. Hayward

# GOD IS DOING
## A NEW THING...
# BECOMING
## A NEW PEOPLE!

*A Lenten Devotional and Study Guide*

Reverend Althea J. Hayward

**To order additional copies of this book, contact:**
Xlibris
844-714-8691
www.Xlibris.com
Orders@Xlibris.com
839437

# CONTENTS

# ACKNOWLEDGMENTS

Thanks to God for the opportunity to exercise one of the gifts given to me for His glory!

Thanks also to my husband of more than 50 years, Dr. Samuel E. Hayward, III, who has loved and supported me throughout our marriage and especially during this project. I am grateful to my daughters, Kimberly and Kristina Hayward for their prayerful encouragement, and to my granddaughter Sydnee Grace Hayward for her joy and love shared throughout this process.

Additional appreciation is extended to my prayer partners, Rev. Dr. Keith Hayward, Evangelist Dorothy Hayward, my pastor, Rev. André P. Jefferson, Sr., and the entire prayer team of the Portsmouth Richmond Roanoke District of the AME Church.

I am especially grateful to my editor, the Rev. Dr. Valdes J. Snipes, for her prayers, encouragement, and editing.

# THE WORD OF GOD

## Devotional Scripture Foundation:

### Isaiah 43:18 – 21 (KJV)

*"Remember ye not the former things, Neither consider the things of old. Behold, **I will do a new thing;** Now it shall spring forth; shall ye not know it? I will even make a way in the wilderness, And rivers in the desert. The beast of the field shall honour me, The dragons and the †owls: Because I give waters in the wilderness, And rivers in the desert, To give drink to my people, my chosen. This people have I formed for myself; They shall shew forth my praise."[1]*

### Isaiah 43:18–21 (NLT)

*"But forget all that— it is nothing compared to what I am going to do. For **I am about to do something new.** See, I have already begun! Do you not see it? I will make a pathway through the wilderness. I will create rivers in the dry wasteland. The wild animals in the fields will thank me, the jackals and owls, too, for giving them water in the desert. Yes, I will make rivers in the dry wasteland so my chosen people can be refreshed. I have made Israel for myself, and they will someday honor me before the whole world."[2]*

---

[1] *The Holy Bible: King James Version*. (2009). (Electronic Edition of the 1900 Authorized Version., Is 43:18–21). Bellingham, WA: Logos Research Systems, Inc.

[2] Holy Bible. (2015). NLT Tyndale House Publishing, Inc.

## Isaiah 43:18-21 (AMP)

*"Do not [earnestly] remember the former things; neither consider the things of old. Behold, **I am doing a new thing**! Now it springs forth; do you not perceive and know it and will you not give heed to it? I will even make a way in the wilderness and rivers in the desert. The beasts of the field honor Me, the jackals and the ostriches, because I give waters in the wilderness and rivers in the desert, to give drink to My people, My chosen, [Isa. 41:17, 18; 48:21.] The people I formed for Myself, that they may set forth My praise [and they shall do it]."* [3]

## 2 Corinthians 5:17 (KJV)

*"Therefore if any man be in Christ, he is a new creature: old things are passed away; behold, all things are become new."* [4]

[3] *The Amplified Bible*. (1987). (Is 43:18–21). La Habra, CA: The Lockman Foundation.

[4] *The Holy Bible: King James Version*. (2009). (Electronic Edition of the 1900 Authorized Version., 2 Co 5:17–Ga 6:15). Bellingham, WA: Logos Research Systems, Inc.

# INTRODUCTION

One of the most exciting features of my secular career was to design and help prepare others to accept change. Change can be exciting or, depending on the circumstances, people involved, and the way change is managed, it can be harrowing. Christianity is all about change; it is a life-long process. We grow from strength to strength. When we stop growing, we must examine why and do something about it.

I was gifted with a beautiful glass music box in an egg shape some time ago. The glass egg had beautiful etchings and was designed in dark red and clear glass colors. But, unfortunately, I was never able to get the music box at the base of the egg to play. You see, the key mechanism to wind up the music box was not working. When I discovered this, I shook the egg. I could hear the parts rattling around inside the egg, but I couldn't reach them. So, for the music box to operate as designed, I needed to send it back to the manufacturer, who would know how to take it apart, fix it, and put it back together again. I didn't have the music box refurbished because I used it in teaching and preaching sessions. I learned a lesson from my music box, which I often share. **<u>We cannot fix ourselves</u>**! We are human and tend to push back from change when that change is necessary but painful. We must be willing to submit ourselves to our "manufacturer," God, Himself for a "makeover."

Beloved, we can begin the change process by acknowledging that we don't know everything about everything! When we accept these truths we open ourselves to dependence on God. Jesus the Christ, then begins a beautiful process in us. Next, it is critical to spend more time at Jesus' feet, cultivating an intimate relationship with our Savior. An amazing transformation occurs as we nurture this relationship by humbling ourselves in prayer and study of God's Word. The personhood of Christ, the mind of Christ, the attitude of Christ, the Will of God, and His unconditional love and favor take over our lives. Are you looking for a teacher, a coach, a motivator? Let's ask the Holy Spirit to guide us through this process. I guarantee you'll love the new you!

## The Genesis of this Devotional:

With the onslaught of COVID-19 and its continuous mutations, we are experiencing a rapidly changing world. Before the CDC and health professionals can dispense vaccines and boosters to stabilize the country's health, another disease or variant of the original Coronavirus appears. Yes, the world is constantly changing and full of challenges. Yet, Jehovah God has made promises to His people in the face of all challenges. His Promises have always brought us hope and renewal. For example, He has promised never to leave nor forsake us. God's Message to us is clear. He stands ready to equip us to be more effective in this ever-changing world. God is doing a New Thing! He wants "New People!" Listen, we are all pandemic-worn, and many Christians have grown weak and discouraged. The good news is that help is available! God needs a revitalized body of believers to evangelize the world in these troubled times. He wants us to experience consistent renewal. This renewal re-aligns our thinking, living, and relationships to comply with God's Word. Beloved, be assured we will make it through this wilderness experience as long as we hold tightly to God. Jesus wants us to follow His example in the wilderness. We will not fail!

It was about 7:15 am, and I had finished my Bible Study that morning. As clear as day, I heard God say to me, "You will write a Lenten Devotional. Start now." He gave me the theme for the study. I sat in my chair dumbfounded for a moment trying to talk myself out of this new task, and then I heard God speak again clearly. He repeated the instruction. I researched the scripture God gave to me and immediately got excited and inspired about this Devotional's potential. I obeyed. You see, beyond any shadow of a doubt, our Father wants us to walk in confidence, knowing that He is working on our behalf. He always has a plan to undergird and refresh us. I pray your life is abundantly enriched and lavishly blessed as you use this Devotional.

## How The Lenten Devotional Is Organized:

Beginning with the first days of Lent and then each week in Lent, a Lenten Meditation Message is offered. The Weekly Message presents the theme or emphasis for the week. The Daily Focus will provide a Spiritual Vitamin complete with a topic, a Scripture, a Prayer, a Thought for the Day to complete the study each day, and a moment for your reflections for today.

## Tools You Will Need:

To benefit from this Lenten Devotional Guide, we suggest you set aside quiet time each day to focus. In addition, we recommend you keep a journal of your thoughts and the revelations God gives to you as you read and study. They will be a blessing to you as God reveals Himself to you during this special and intimate time with Him. If you do not have a journal, feel free to use a notebook. The importance of recording your experience is what we are emphasizing. Later, when you review your journal entries, you will be blessed to see your progress on your journey to re-birth and renewal.

## Group Use of the Devotional Guide:

While this Lenten Devotional Guide is designed for individual use, it can be used as a resource tool for group Bible Study and discussion during the Lenten Season. For group study, try setting up teams to discuss the weekly Message, the scriptures, and thoughts for the day. Encourage a reporting out of your team findings at the end of their work time. Make it fun! Make it meaningful! Be sure to highlight significant outcomes and discoveries; encourage members to share how the experience is impacting them.

May the richness of God's Word bless and rejuvenate your life. May each of us experience restoration! We pray this Lenten Devotional will help reposition you in the Perfect Will of God! He is doing a New Thing in this Post-Pandemic Era!

**GOD IS DOING A NEW THING. WE ARE BECOMING A NEW PEOPLE!**

# ASH WEDNESDAY

---

## Historical Statement

Observed by the Christian Church, Ash Wednesday is the first day of Lent, occurring six and a half weeks before Easter. Ash Wednesday is celebrated as a solemn reminder of the world's need for reconciliation with God and marks the beginning of the penitential Lenten season. It is commonly observed with the application of ashes and fasting.

In the early Christian Church, the length of the Lenten celebration varied, but eventually, it began six weeks (42 days) before Easter. The original Lenten observation provided only thirty-six days of fasting (excluding Sundays). The First Council of Nicaea spoke of Lent as a period of fasting for forty days in preparation for Eastertide. They added four days before the first Sunday in Lent to establish forty fasting days, imitating Jesus Christ's fasting in the wilderness.

In early Rome, it was the practice for penitents and grievous sinners to begin their period of public penance on the first day of Lent in preparation for their restoration to the sacrament of the Eucharist. They were sprinkled with ashes, dressed in sackcloth, and obliged to remain apart until they were reconciled with the Christian community on Maundy Thursday, the Thursday before

Easter. When these practices fell into disuse (8th–10th century), the beginning of the penitential season of Lent was symbolized by placing ashes on the heads of the entire congregation.

In the modern Roman Catholic Church and many Protestant churches observing Ash Wednesday, the ashes obtained by burning the palms used on the previous Palm Sunday are applied in the shape of a cross on the forehead of each worshipper on Ash Wednesday. Together with Good Friday (which marks the crucifixion of Jesus before Easter), Ash Wednesday is a day of fasting and abstinence. It has been the practice of many to abstain from a habit or food during Lent, beginning on Ash Wednesday.

The Church directly associates ashes with repentance. In ancient times ashes were used to express grief or sorrow. For example, when her half-brother raped her, Tamar sprinkled ashes on her head, tore her robe, and with her face buried in her hands went away crying" (2 Samuel 13:19). The gesture was also used to express sorrow for sins and faults. In Job 42:5–6, Job says to God: "I have heard of thee by the hearing of the ear: but now mine eye seeth thee. Wherefore I abhor myself, and repent in dust and ashes." The prophet Jeremiah calls for repentance by saying: "O daughter of my people, gird on sackcloth, roll in the ashes" (Jer 6:26). The prophet Daniel recounted pleading to God: "I turned to the Lord God, pleading in earnest prayer, with fasting, sackcloth and ashes" (Daniel 9:3). Jesus speaks of the practice in Matthew 11:21 and Luke 10:13: "If the mighty works done in you had been done in Tyre and Sidon, they would have repented long ago (sitting) in sackcloth and ashes."

*(Excerpted from the Editors of Encyclopaedia Britannica and updated by Melissa Petruzzello –https://www.britannica. com/topic/Ash-Wednesday-Christian-holy-day)*

# Devotional Hymn

## "I AM THINE, O LORD"
### (Fanny J. Crosby, William H. Doane)

I am Thine, O Lord, I have heard Thy voice,
And it told Thy love to me;
But I long to rise in the arms of faith,
And be closer drawn to Thee.

2

Consecrate me now to Thy service, Lord,
By the pow'r of grace divine;
Let my soul look up with a steadfast hope,
And my will be lost in Thine.

3

O the pure delight of a single hour
That before Thy throne I spend,
When I kneel in prayer, and with Thee, my God,
I commune as friend with friend!

4

There are depths of love that I yet may know
Ere Thee face to face I see;
There are heights of joy that I yet may reach
Ere I rest in Peace with Thee.

Chorus
Draw me nearer, nearer, blessed Lord,
To the cross where Thou hast died;
Draw me nearer, nearer, nearer, blessed Lord,
To Thy precious, bleeding side.

AMEN!

# Ash Wednesday Meditation

### "WASH ME, PLEASE!"

*Psalm 51:1-3 (NLT)*
*"Have mercy on me, O God, because of your unfailing love. Because of your great compassion, blot out the stain of my sins. Wash me clean from my guilt. Purify me from my sin. For I recognize my rebellion; it haunts me day and night."*

How many times have you felt guilty about something you've said, done, or thought? If you have never felt guilty about anything, then there may be something wrong with you, my friend! Every one of us has experienced guilt about something! But, unfortunately, we live in a world where it is almost impossible to exist without offending or hurting somebody. Remember, we are all human, born in sin and shaped in iniquity (Psalm 51:5). So, we must be sensitive to others as we move about our communities. And, when we offend, it is wise to seek forgiveness immediately.

Christmas and Thanksgiving holidays are exciting times at our house. One of the essential preparation jobs involves decorating the dining room table. These special occasions call for the use of silverware, glassware, and dishes we do not use regularly. The preparation time is quite a production! The plates and glassware are thoroughly washed. The silverware is polished, and we set the table for our enjoyment. Of course, we want the best on the table! Who would dare put dirty, dusty dishes from the china cabinet on the table? You see, it's a new season, a unique season of celebration. God's Word reminds us we are His vessels. We are His people, and He is initiating a transition to a new season. He desires to use us in this new season. Our priority must be to get washed up, cleaned up!

Because of God's unfailing love, we have access to forgiveness for **every** single sin, whether they are sins of omission or commission.

God wants us free of the soil of sin and guilt. So, come on, let's wash up! Let's acknowledge how we have rebelled against Him and repent. Because of His great compassion, God is willing to wipe out the stain of our sin and guilt. We no longer have to carry the weight of guilt! Isn't that remarkable? What a mighty God we serve!

**SONG: "THERE IS A FOUNTAIN FILLED WITH BLOOD" (William Cowper)**

**PRAYER:** Dear Lord and Father of Mankind, forgive my foolish ways. Re-clothe me in my rightful mind. I confess my sins and failures and I thank You for the blessing of forgiveness. Thank you, Father, for the precious blood of Your beloved Son, Jesus the Christ, that blots out every stain and erases all my self-reproach. I Thank You. Your love and compassion wash me anew. Thank You for the Peace Your forgiveness brings to my heart and life. For this, I love and thank You in Jesus' Name. AMEN!

**TODAY'S THOUGHT: Lord, I confess I need to be free! Please wash me over again!**

**My reflections for Today:**_____
_____
_____
_____
_____

# Thursday Focus

### Spiritual Vitamin: Give Me A Clean Heart And The Right Attitude!

**PSALM 51:10-11 (MSG)**
*"God, make a fresh start in me, shape a Genesis week from the chaos of my life. Don't throw me out with the trash or fail to breathe holiness in me. Bring me back from gray exile; put a fresh wind in my sails!"*

**SONG: "GIVE ME A CLEAN HEART" (Dr. Margaret Douroux, Ph.D., Composer)**

> "Give me a clean heart so that I may serve Thee.
> Lord, fix my heart so that I may be used by Thee.
> For I'm not worthy of all these blessings
> Give me a clean heart, and I'll follow Thee."

**PRAYER:** Heavenly Father, we give you thanks for another day. Thank you for Your mercies which are new every morning. We stand before You today, requesting that You grant us a fresh start. Please do a "new thing" in us; shape a Genesis week from the chaos of our lives. Breathe in us afresh and fashion our minds and attitudes so that they mirror those of Your Son, Jesus Christ. It is in Jesus' Name we pray, Amen and Amen.

**THOUGHT FOR THE DAY: I am on a mission to shape a Genesis week from the chaos of my life.**

My reflections for today: _____

_____

_____

_____

# Friday Focus

**Spiritual Vitamin: I am longing for restoration.**

### Psalm 51: 12-13 (NLT)

*"Restore to me the joy of Your Salvation, and make me willing to obey you. Then I will teach your ways to rebels, and they will return to you."*

## SONG: "LORD JESUS, I LONG TO BE PERFECTLY WHOLE" (James Nicholson)

Lord Jesus, I long to be perfectly whole; I
want Thee forever to live in my soul,
Break down every idol, cast out every foe; Now
wash me, and I shall be whiter than snow.

Lord Jesus, look down from Thy throne in the skies, And help
me to make a complete sacrifice; I give up myself, and whatever
I know, Now wash me, and I shall be whiter than snow.

Lord Jesus, for this I most humbly entreat, I
wait, blessed Lord, at Thy crucified feet;
By faith, for my cleansing, I see Thy blood flow, Now
wash me, and I shall be whiter than snow.

Lord Jesus, Thou see-est I patiently wait, Come
now, and within me a new heart create;
To those who have sought Thee, Thou never saidst "No,"
Now wash me, and I shall be whiter than snow.

## Chorus

Whiter than snow, Yes, whiter than snow.
Now wash me, and I shall be whiter than snow.

**PRAYER:** Dear Father, thank you for the Joy of Your Salvation! How wonderful it is to experience restoration in Your Presence! Thank you for cleansing us! We give ourselves to You all over again. Use us as You will today, and every day, in Jesus' Name, we pray, Amen.

**TODAY'S THOUGHT: We are made perfectly whole because of the blood of Jesus – what joy that gives us!**

**My reflections for Today:**_____

_____

_____

_____

_____

# SATURDAY FOCUS

**Spiritual Vitamin: Hang in there! God is Faithful!**

**Lamentations 3:21-24 (NLT)**
*"Yet there is one ray of hope:His compassion never ends. It is only the Lord's mercies that have kept us from complete destruction. Great is His faithfulness; his loving-kindness begins afresh each day. My soul claims the Lord as my inheritance; therefore, I will hope in Him."*

**SONG: "Great is Thy Faithfulness" (William M. Runyan / Thomas O Chisholm / Eric Allyn Schrotenboer)**

Great is Thy faithfulness, O God my Father
There is no shadow of turning with Thee
Thou changest not, Thy compassions, they fail not
As Thou hast been, Thou forever will be

2

Summer and winter and springtime and harvest
Sun, moon and stars in their courses above
Join with all nature in manifold witness
To Thy great faithfulness, mercy and love

3

Pardon for sin and a peace that endureth
Thine own dear presence to cheer and to guide
Strength for today and bright hope for tomorrow
Blessings all mine with ten thousand beside

Chorus
Great is Thy faithfulness; Great is Thy faithfulness
Morning by morning, new mercies I see
All I have needed Thy hand hath provided
Great is Thy faithfulness, Lord, unto me

**PRAYER:** Father, I need your help today. Things are pretty challenging right now, but I am so glad that Your Word reminds me of Your love for me. You prove it by Your faithfulness to me each day. So please help me slow down and take one day at a time. Help me remember that you give us brand new mercies each day, and I can make it today with the strength you provide me. Thank You for this comforting realization in Jesus' name, AMEN.

**TODAY'S THOUGHT: Don't Stress! We Are The Beneficiaries Of God's Faithfulness And Mercy Each And Every Day!**

**My reflections for Today:**_____
_____
_____
_____
_____

MY SINCERE COMMITMENT:

I WILL <u>NOT</u> ALLOW THE ADVERSARY
TO STEAL MY POSITION AS A CHOSEN
VESSEL OF GOD! I HAVE BEEN
WASHED IN THE BLOOD OF THE LAMB!
SATAN HAS <u>NOT</u> HAD THIS PRIVILEGE
AND NEVER WILL!

# FIRST SUNDAY IN LENT - WEEKLY MEDITATION

---

## Don't Fret! It's A Setup!

**SCRIPTURE: St. Luke 4:1-2 (NLT)**

*"Then Jesus, full of the Holy Spirit, returned from the Jordan River. He was led by the Spirit in the wilderness, ² where he was tempted by the devil for forty days. Jesus ate nothing all that time and became very hungry."*

We were delighted! We just paid off the last car note. So we were free from car payments. Euphoric about this, we decided to take a trip to celebrate the fact we were free of debt. My husband decided to take the "travel car" to get serviced as we planned our trip. Although wouldn't you know it, there were quite a few things on the vehicle requiring attention. So we decided to cancel the travel and spend the money on the car repairs. After the excitement and celebration of paying off the car note and planning a trip, it was not very encouraging. In retrospect, however, we were thankful we had the car repaired. You see, some of the items needing attention would have been more expensive had we put off the repairs.

Luke gives the account of the Baptism of Jesus. He notes when Jesus was baptized, the Spirit of God visually descended on Him in the form of a dove. Next, he describes God speaking and pronouncing His signal approval of Jesus. The Bible notes the Holy Spirit then <u>led</u> Jesus into a wilderness experience! After experiencing a God-moment, Jesus is now prepared to be tested in the wilderness. How awesome this is! How many times have we experienced God pouring Himself into us, and then that power transfer is followed by a testing or challenging period? **It's called a setup!**

Here's the good news! **Whenever God leads us into a wilderness experience, we can be confident that He has already designed the victorious outcome**! Isn't that wonderful! Just as God believed in Jesus, He believes in us. How we see ourselves and how we handle ourselves during the wilderness experience (the test) determines our victory. We must see ourselves as God sees us. We were purchased by the blood of Jesus and stamped as His. Our names are written in the palms of His hands. God believes in us! Therefore, any tests have already been fixed for us to pass. We cannot be defeated so long as we trust and hold on to the God of our Salvation. Therefore, every setup is an opportunity for God to demonstrate victory in our lives – that's hope! Hallelujah!

**PRAYER:** Heavenly Father, thank You for another day. Your Word instructs us to be thankful in all things, including those things that appear to be challenging. We are grateful You have already provided victory for your children in every wilderness experience. Help us walk in faith and victory today and every day in Jesus' name, Amen.

**TODAY'S THOUGHT: Don't give up! Don't give in! Most of all, don't compromise your divine destiny. <u>Remember, in every challenge, Jesus has already guaranteed your victory!</u>**

**My reflections for Today:**_____

_____

_____

_____

_____

# First Week – Monday Focus

## Spiritual Vitamin: Hold on to Your Identity in Christ!

### Luke 4:3-4(NLT)

*"Then the devil said to him, "If you are the Son of God, tell this stone to become a loaf of bread. But Jesus told him, "No! The Scriptures say, 'People do not live by bread alone."*

### HYMN – "I AM THINE O LORD"

**PRAYER:** Heavenly Father, thank you for the unique identity given to me in Christ Jesus! You designed me for specific Kingdom purposes, and I am grateful that You are doing a new thing in me. Please forgive me for my shortcomings and help me always to remember who and whose I am. In my uniqueness, don't allow me to compare myself or the gifts You've given me with others. Thank You for placing Your Word in my heart so I can respond with authority to temptation, in Jesus' name, Amen.

**TODAY'S THOUGHT: Never allow others the liberty of defining who you are! Only God and you have that authority! So today, remember <u>who</u> and <u>whose</u> you are!**

**My reflections for Today:**_____

_____

_____

_____

_____

# FIRST WEEK – TUESDAY FOCUS

### Spiritual Vitamin: No Discussion! I Am Trusting God With My Life!

**Matthew 4:5-7 (GNT)**

*"Then the Devil took Jesus to Jerusalem, the Holy City, set him on the highest point of the Temple, and said to him, "If you are God's Son, throw yourself down, for the scripture says, 'God will give orders to his angels about you; they will hold you up with their hands so that not even your feet will be hurt on the stones.'" Jesus answered, "But the scripture also says, 'Do not put the Lord your God to the test.'"*

**SONG: "MY HOPE IS BUILT" (Edward Mote, William B. Bradbury)**

**PRAYER:** Heavenly Father, Savior of Mankind, thank You for reminding me through Your Word that I can trust you with every area of my life. Give me the strength and wisdom to make decisions that continue to build my faith in You. Today, please manifest Your Presence in my life and help me be a reflection of You in the world, in Jesus' name, AMEN!

**TODAY'S THOUGHT: I Am Determined To Trust God In Everything – No Discussion!**

**My reflections for Today:**_____

_____

_____

_____

_____

# First Week – Wednesday Focus

**Spiritual Vitamin: I am created to worship
God in Spirit and in Truth!**

**Matthew 4:8-10 (NLT)**
*"Next, the devil took him to the peak of a very high mountain and showed him all the kingdoms of the world and their glory. "I will give it all to you," he said, "if you will kneel down and worship me." "Get out of here, Satan," Jesus told him. "For the Scriptures say, 'You must worship the Lord your God and serve only him.'"*

**SONG: "I WORSHIP YOU BECAUSE OF WHO YOU ARE!
"(Brian Kelly McKnight & Michael Brandon Barnes)**

> Because of who you are, I give you glory, Because of who you are, I give you praise
> Because of who you are, I will lift my voice and say, Lord, I worship you because of who you are Lord, I worship you because of who you are.
>
> Jehovah Jireh, my provider, Jehovah Nissi, Lord, You reign in victory
> Jehovah Shalom, my Prince of Peace, And I worship because of who you are.

**PRAYER:** Dear God, I give you praise and glory! You are full of majesty and might! You are an awesome God. It gives me such joy to worship You. I bless Your Name forever. You are Jehovah Jireh, Jehovah Shalom, Jehovah Shamah, El Elyon, and El Shaddai in my life! You are my provider, my Peace, my healer, my Lord, and my God. Father, You are my everything! Help me be an authentic worshipper, not just with my lips, but by the attitude I exemplify and by the life that I live. Please be glorified in me in Jesus' name, Amen.

**TODAY'S THOUGHT: Don't Be Fooled By Counterfeit Worship Invitations! <u>God Is The Only Target Of Our Worship!</u>**

**My reflections for Today:**_____

_____

_____

_____

_____

# First Week – Thursday Focus

**Spiritual Vitamin: Divine Battle Strategy- God's Complete Restoration Is Always Available After The Battle!**

**MATTHEW 4:11 (NLT)**
*"Then the devil went away, and angels came and took care of Jesus."*

**SONG: "ANGELS WATCHING OVER ME" (Otis Leon McCoy)**

> All night, all day, The angels, keep a watching over
> me (my Lord)
> All night, all day, The angels, keep a watching, over me

**PRAYER:** Father in Heaven, thanks for Your abiding Love and Presence. It protects and keeps us despite every challenge we face. The adversary retreats when he comes up against the hedge of protection and love You place around us. Thanks for Your ongoing care, Your security, and everlasting Peace, Amen!

**TODAY'S THOUGHT: Have No Fear! God Is Near!**

**My reflections for Today:** _____

_____

_____

_____

_____

# FIRST WEEK – FRIDAY FOCUS

**Spiritual Vitamin: God Gets The Last Word! Oh Yes, He Does!**

**SCRIPTURE: 1 PETER 4:8-11 (MSG)**
*"Keep a cool head. Stay alert. The devil is **poised to pounce**, and would like nothing better than to catch you napping. Keep your guard up. You're not the only ones plunged into these hard times. It's the same with Christians all over the world. **<u>So keep a firm grip on the faith</u>**. The suffering won't last forever. It won't be long before this generous God who has great plans for us in Christ—eternal and glorious plans they are!—will have you put together and on your feet for good. He gets the last Word; yes, He does."*

**SONG: "WE'VE COME THIS FAR BY FAITH!" (Albert Goodson)**

> We've come this far by faith, leaning on the Lord, Trusting in His Holy Word. He's never failed us yet. Singin' oh, oh, oh, can't turn around. We've come this far by faith.

> Just the other day, I heard a man say He didn't believe in God's Word. But I can truly say that God has made a way, And He's never failed me yet.

> Don't be discouraged with the troubles in your life. He'll bear your burdens, remove all misery and strife.

**PRAYER:** Dear God, I know You have great plans for me. I want to walk in Your Perfect Will for my life. So help me be on alert and make wise decisions, leaning entirely on Your Guidance and Your Will. I declare I will keep my guard up and keep a firm grip on my faith in You, Father, despite these difficult times. I pray this I in the precious name of Jesus, my Lord, Amen.

**TODAY'S THOUGHT: God Has Plans For Me! And, He Always Has The Last Word!**

**My reflections for Today:**_____

_____

_____

_____

_____

# First Week – Saturday Focus

## Spiritual Vitamin: My Challenges Do Not Define Me! God Has Defined Who I Am, And I Trust Him!

**SCRIPTURE: Ephesians 6:10 (AMP)**
*"In conclusion, be strong in the Lord, draw your strength from Him and be empowered through your union with Him, and in the power of His boundless might."*

**SONG: "Blessed be the Name of the Lord" (Clinton Utterbach)**

> Blessed be the name of the Lord, Blessed be the name of the Lord,
> Blessed be the name of the Lord Most High! (Repeat)
> The name of the Lord is a strong tower, The righteous run into it, And they are saved. (Repeat)

**PRAYER**: Dear Father, thank You for being El Shaddai, our Almighty God! Praise Your Name! Help me hold tightly to Your hand so I may receive Your Strength today and every day. Thank You for the Blessed Holy Spirit who leads and guides me to the Truth. Thank You for Jesus, Your Son, our Savior, and our Redeemer. I am grateful to know You as Abba Father because of Him, and I am joint-heir with Him. Bless me this day to be a blessing to others; in Jesus' name, I pray, AMEN.

**TODAY'S THOUGHT: Christ Is In Me! That's The Hope Of Glory! I Know Who I Am!**

**My reflections for Today:**_____

_____

_____

_____

_____

MY SINCERE COMMITMENT:

I WILL <u>NOT</u> ALLOW THE ADVERSARY
TO STEAL MY POSITION AS A CHOSEN
VESSEL OF GOD! I HAVE BEEN
WASHED IN THE BLOOD OF THE LAMB!
SATAN HAS <u>NOT</u> HAD THIS PRIVILEGE
AND NEVER WILL!

# SECOND SUNDAY IN LENT - WEEKLY MEDITATION

---

## "Doing God's Will…One Day At A Time!"

**SCRIPTURE: Acts 9:3-6 (KJV)**

*"And as he journeyed, he came near Damascus: and suddenly there shined round about him a light from heaven: And he fell to the earth and heard a voice saying unto him, Saul, Saul, why persecutest thou me? And he said, Who art thou, Lord? And the Lord said, I am Jesus whom thou persecutest: it is hard for thee to kick against the pricks. And he trembling and astonished said, <u>Lord, what wilt thou have me to do</u>? And the Lord said unto him, Arise, and go into the city, <u>and it shall be told thee what thou must do.</u>"*

Are you one of those people who often set out to put together a piece of furniture or a toy without the instructions? Some folks are gifted enough to do that, but not regular folks like us. As a result, we usually ended up with a piece on backwards, or we would look on the floor and find a few screws or nails that hadn't been used in the assembly. We were then challenged to go back, study the instructions, and see where we went wrong. It was a struggle!

In this scripture, Saul had been rigorously persecuting Christians. Yet, God sees qualities in Saul that can build and advance the Kingdom of God. He desired to use Saul's energy, enthusiasm, and intelligence to evangelize. So, I guess you could say that Saul had a face-to-face encounter with God on the Damascus Road. After Saul falls to the ground, God confronts him about his persecution of the Church. When engaged by God, Saul immediately surrenders his will to God. His immediate question to God is: "What will you have me to do?" Are you willing to ask God that question and then follow with childlike faith to carry out His instructions? I sure hope so.

In the Bible Study, Experiencing God by Henry and Richard Blackaby, and Claude King, we are taught how to know and do the Will of God. One of the most pertinent points made in the study is we must embrace God's Will as our own. In other words, when we surrender our lives to God, we must understand we yield ourselves to His complete management and direction. It is critical to learn we must do things His way. Guess what? We do this one day and one moment at a time! We can become overwhelmed quickly as new converts if we attempt to do everything others ask of us. After all, we do not have the overall divine plan; God does! He has invited us to join Him in His work! How about asking Him what He wants us to do. Let's seek His divine and perfect Will for our lives. I challenge you to follow Saul's example and ask God, "what will you have me to do." **I know He will answer.** He will open up His Will for you, reveal your assignment, and, in fact, "change your name."

**PRAYER:** Lord God, You are an awesome God! Just as you meticulously created every aspect and component of this world, you also created me. Thank You for designing me to accomplish a particular role and task that is a part of Your Perfect Will. Father, forgive me for the times when I have followed my own thoughts and ways. Please keep me focused and centered in Your plan for my life. Help me seek You each day for my assignment and follow You at all times, in Jesus' name, AMEN!

**TODAY'S THOUGHT: God Invited Me To Join Him In His Work Today. I Am Determined To Do His Perfect Will, One Day At A Time.**

# Second Week

## SONG: "THY WAY, O LORD, NOT MINE" (Nina B. Jackson)

Thy way, O Lord, not Mine, Thy will be done, not mine;
Since Thou for me did bleed, And now doth intercede,
Each day I simply plead, Thy will be done.

Thy way, O Lord, not Mine, Let glory all be Thine;
Keep me, lest I may stray, Near Thee from day to day;
Teach me to watch and pray, Thy will be done.

Hide me from self, O Lord, May I attend Thy word;
Send pride beyond recall, Let each assailer fall,
Be Thou my all in all, Thy will be done.

Submissively I bow; With strength and grace endow
This weary, sinful heart; Shield from each cruel dart;
May I from Thee ne'er part, Thy will be done.

REFRAIN:
Thy Will, Thy Will be done, Thy Will, Thy Will be done;
Incline my heart each day to say,
Thy Will be done!

**My reflections for Today:** _____
_____
_____
_____
_____

# SECOND WEEK – MONDAY FOCUS

## Spiritual Vitamin: Self-Denial Is One Of The Requirements To Do God's Will

**SCRIPTURE: LUKE 22:41-44 (NLT)**
*"He walked away, about a stone's throw, and knelt down and prayed, "Father, if you are willing, please take this cup of suffering away from me. **Yet I want Your will to be done, not Mine.**" Then an angel from heaven appeared and strengthened him. He prayed more fervently, and he was in such agony of spirit that his sweat fell to the ground like great drops of blood."*

**SONG: THY WAY, O LORD, NOT MINE**

**PRAYER:** Dear Lord, I thank you for hearing me. I honor You because You love me and tune Your ears to my prayers. I pray You will shape my will and my desires to conform them to Your plan for my life. Please capture my every passion and use it for Your purposes and glory in Jesus' name, AMEN.

**TODAY'S THOUGHT: Christ Is My Example Of Self-Denial. I Am Following His Model.**

My reflections for Today:_____
_____
_____
_____
_____

# SECOND WEEK – TUESDAY FOCUS

### Spiritual Vitamin: God's Will Is What Is Best For Us

## SCRIPTURE: JOHN 6:35-40 (NLT)

*"Jesus replied, "I am the bread of life. Whoever comes to Me will never be hungry again. Whoever believes in Me will never be thirsty. But you haven't believed in Me even though you have seen Me. However, those the Father has given Me will come to Me, and I will never reject them. For I have come down from heaven <u>to do the will of God who sent Me, not to do My own will</u>. And this is the will of God, that I should not lose even one of all those He has given Me, but that I should raise them up at the last day. <u>For it is My Father's will that all who see His Son and believe in Him should have eternal life</u>. I will raise them up at the last day."*

## SONG: "THY WAY, O LORD, NOT MINE"

**PRAYER**: Heavenly Father, we praise you for making provision for our reconciliation through Jesus Christ! Thank You for your love. Your Word declares that it is not Your Will for any of us to be lost. Help us to surrender to Your Will continuously. We appreciate Jesus' investment in our eternal salvation. Praise His Holy name forever, AMEN!

## TODAY'S THOUGHT: God's Will And Way Yield Eternal Dividends!

**My reflections for Today:**_____

_____

_____

_____

_____

# Second Week – Wednesday Focus

**Spiritual Vitamin: Sacrifice Your Life To God As An Offering!**

**SCRIPTURE: Romans 12:1 – 2 (MSG)**

*"So here's what I want you to do, God helping you: Take your everyday, ordinary life—your sleeping, eating, going-to-work, and walking-around life—and place it before God as an offering. Embracing what God does for you is the best thing you can do for him. Don't become so well-adjusted to your culture that you fit into it without even thinking. Instead, fix your attention on God. You'll be changed from the inside out. Readily recognize what he wants from you, and quickly respond to it. Unlike the culture around you, always dragging you down to its level of immaturity, God brings the best out of you, develops well-formed maturity in you."*

**SONG: "THY WAY, O LORD, NOT MINE"**

**PRAYER:** Dear Father, I give myself to you. Take every component of my life and use it for Your glory. Father, fix my attention on Your Will for my life. Change me from the inside out, and help me respond quickly to Your direction, in Jesus' name, AMEN!

**TODAY'S THOUGHT: The World's Culture Does Not Fit Us. We Are Being Transformed And Shaped For Greater Things!**

**My reflections for Today:**_____

_____

_____

_____

_____

# SECOND WEEK – THURSDAY FOCUS

**Spiritual Vitamin: News Bulletin! The World Is Passing Away!**

## SCRIPTURE: 1 JOHN 2:15-17 (AMP)

*"Do not love the world [of sin that opposes God and His precepts], nor the things that are in the world. If anyone loves the world, the love of the Father is not in him. For all that is in the world—the lust and sensual craving of the flesh and the lust and longing of the eyes and the boastful pride of life [pretentious confidence in one's resources or in the stability of earthly things]—these do not come from the Father, but are from the world. The world is passing away, and with it its lusts [the shameful pursuits and ungodly longings]; but the one who does the will of God and carries out His purposes lives forever."*

## SONG: "THY WAY, O LORD, NOT MINE!"

**PRAYER:** Dear God, thank you for reminding us that we do not belong to this world as Your children. You have reminded us that we will live forever if we do Your Will and carry out Your purposes. So, today, help us earnestly seek Your Will in all that we say and do so that we bring honor to you, in Jesus' name, AMEN!

**TODAY'S THOUGHT: The World Is On Life Support. We Choose To Bring Honor To God By Doing His Will!**

**My reflections for Today:** _____
_____
_____
_____
_____

# Second Week – Friday Focus

## Spiritual Vitamin: I'm Committed To God's Will For The Long Haul!

**SCRIPTURE: COLOSSIANS 1:9-12 (MSG)**

*"Be assured that from the first day we heard of you, we haven't stopped praying for you, asking God to give you wise minds and spirits attuned to his will, and so acquire a thorough understanding of the ways in which God works. We pray that you'll live well for the Master, making him proud of you as you work hard in his orchard. As you learn more and more how God works, you will learn how to do your work. We pray that you'll have the strength to stick it out over the long haul—not the grim strength of gritting your teeth, but the glory-strength God gives. It is strength that endures the unendurable and spills over into joy, thanking the Father who makes us strong enough to take part in everything bright and beautiful that he has for us."*

**SONG: "THY WAY, O LORD, NOT MINE!"**

**PRAYER**: Heavenly Father, thank you for those who are praying with and for me. I desire to live well for You, Lord, and bear much fruit. I am making a total commitment to You, Lord. I have nothing to lose and everything to gain. I surrender my will to You again. Empower me to do Your work, in Jesus' name, AMEN!

**TODAY'S THOUGHT: My Commitment To God Provides Glory-Strength To Carry Out His Will!**

**My reflections for Today:**_____

_____

_____

_____

_____

# SECOND WEEK – SATURDAY FOCUS

### Spiritual Vitamin: I Have Confidence, Strength & Fortitude – I'm Hanging In There!

**SCRIPTURE: HEBREWS 10:35-36 (NLT)**
*"So do not throw away this confident trust in the Lord. Remember the great reward it brings you! [36] Patient endurance is what you need now so that you will continue to do God's will. Then you will receive all that he has promised."*

**SONG: "THY WAY, O LORD, NOT MINE!"**

**PRAYER:** Father in Heaven, thank you for another day and another chance to get closer to You. I am grateful that you give me confidence and faith in Your Word and Your Will. Lord, I know You are with me. With You leading me, I know I can do all things. Therefore, I am determined to hold on to what You've taught me. May Your Will be done in me, in Jesus' name, AMEN!

**TODAY'S THOUGHT: God's Will, God's Way, God's Plan - - I'm All In!**

**My reflections for Today:** _____
_____
_____
_____
_____

MY SINCERE COMMITMENT:

I WILL <u>NOT</u> ALLOW THE ADVERSARY
TO STEAL MY POSITION AS A CHOSEN
VESSEL OF GOD!  I HAVE BEEN
WASHED IN THE BLOOD OF THE LAMB!
SATAN HAS <u>NOT</u> HAD THIS PRIVILEGE
AND NEVER WILL!

# THIRD SUNDAY IN LENT - WEEKLY MEDITATION

---

## "Give Yourself A Gift - - Forgive, For Real!"

**SCRIPTURE: MATTHEW 6:10-14 (GNT)**

*"May your holy name be honored; may your Kingdom come; may your will be done on earth as it is in heaven. Give us today the food we need. Forgive us the wrongs we have done, as we forgive the wrongs that others have done to us. Do not bring us to hard testing, but keep us safe from the Evil One." ¹⁴ "If you forgive others the wrongs they have done to you, your Father in heaven will also forgive you. ¹⁵ But if you do not forgive others, then your Father will not forgive the wrongs you have done."*

As a clergyperson for thirty years, and the spouse of a Methodist pastor for more than fifty years, I cannot tell you how many people I have counseled who were consumed with anger and bitterness about an offense they experienced and couldn't get over. In some cases, folks could not even remember the origin of the misunderstanding. I remember an old movie/mini-series,

"The Hatfields and the McCoys." They were two families from West Virginia and Kentucky, feuding families I called them. Unfortunately, unforgiveness simply led to a permanent state of misery, hatred, and dislike among them.

In giving us an outline for prayer, Jesus teaches us to ask God to "forgive the wrongs we have done, as we forgive the wrongs that others have done to us." We say this each time we repeat the Lord's Prayer. "And, forgive us our debts as we forgive those who trespass against us" is the request we repeat each time we recite this prayer. Here is what we are asking God to do: To the degree that I forgive those who trespass against me, Lord, by that same measure, please forgive me." Scary, isn't it! You see, we want God's forgiveness for all the wrongs we do but are somehow unwilling to forgive other people for the evil they do to us! The Bible declares that if you forgive others for their wrongdoing, God in heaven <u>will also forgive you</u>.

We benefit from acts of forgiveness, and the reality is that forgiveness helps us remain healthy spiritually, psychologically, emotionally, and physically. Doctors and Psychologists have suggested that forgiveness of others and self puts us back in the "driver's seat," freeing us to take control of our psychological, emotional, and physical health while allowing us to accept the gift of power and strength that forgiveness provides.

Forgiveness is a gift! It is the gift that also benefits the person who wronged us. Forgiving others releases those persons to God for handling. He will, in due season, take care of the issues. It doesn't mean we are weak. It means we trust God to handle our business! Listen, we are human and prone to mistakes and wrongdoing. If we ever want to be forgiven by others, we need to demonstrate forgiveness and mercy ourselves. After all, didn't Jesus do that for us?

**PRAYER:** Lord God, I confess and repent of all my sins and failures. Thank you for forgiveness, for giving me another opportunity and a clean slate! What a loving God you are! You have made it clear that the blood of Jesus has washed all my sins away, and I am free! Thank you for your mercy. Please help me be merciful and forgiving of others, in Jesus' name, AMEN!

**TODAY'S THOUGHT: Follow Jesus' Example. Forgive, And Do It Quickly!**

# Third Week

## SONG: JUST A LITTLE TALK WITH JESUS (Cleavant Derricks)

I once was lost in sin, but Jesus took me in,
And then a little light from heaven filled my soul;
It bathed my heart in love, and wrote my name above,
And just a little talk with Jesus made me whole.

Sometimes my path seems drear, without a ray of cheer,
And then a cloud of doubt may hide the light of day;
The mists of sin may rise and hide the starry skies,
But just a little talk with Jesus clears the way.

I may have doubts and fear; my eyes be filled with tears,
But Jesus is a friend who watches day and night;
I go to Him in prayer; He knows my every care,
And just a little talk with Jesus makes it right.

Refrain:
Now let us – Have a little talk with Jesus,
Let us – tell Him all about our troubles,
He will – hear our faintest cry,
And He will – answer by and by,
Now when you – feel a little prayer wheel turning,
And you – know a little fire is burning
You will – find a little talk with Jesus makes it right.

**My reflections for Today:**_____

_____

_____

_____

_____

# Third Week – Monday Focus

## Spiritual Vitamin: With the kindness and compassion of Christ, I forgive!

### SCRIPTURE: EPHESIANS 4:31-32 (NIV)

*"Get rid of all bitterness, rage and anger, brawling and slander, along with every form of malice. Be kind and compassionate to one another, forgiving each other, just as in Christ God forgave you."*

### SONG: "BLEST BE THE TIE THAT BINDS" (John Fawcett)

Blest be the tie that binds Our hearts in Christian love;
The fellowship of kindred minds Is like to that above.

**PRAYER:** Dear Lord, thank You for another day and for the Christ-like compassion with which You are filling me each day. I dedicate myself anew to Your principles of love and forgiveness. Father, help me rid myself of anger and bitterness and forgive others. Please give me the strength to let go of my pride and embrace more of Christ's qualities of love and compassion in Jesus' name, AMEN.

**TODAY'S THOUGHT: Forgiveness is a gift. Make sure you give it to someone today!**

**My reflections for Today:**_____
_____
_____
_____
_____

# Third Week – Tuesday Focus

**Spiritual Vitamin: Our assignment is to reflect God in the world – to be merciful and forgive!**

**SCRIPTURE: Luke 6:36 & 37 (NIV)**
*"Be merciful, just as your Father is merciful. Do not judge, and you will not be judged. Do not condemn, and you will not be condemned. Forgive, and you will be forgiven."*

**SONG: "YOUR GRACE & MERCY" (Franklin Williams)**

> Your grace and mercy brought me through. I'm living
> this moment because of You.
> I want to thank You and praise You too. Your grace
> and mercy brought me through.

**PRAYER:** Heavenly Father, thank You for the mercy and grace You have extended to me throughout my life. Your Word clearly states that You did not come into the world to condemn but to save. Help me reflect that same grace and mercy to others as I live from day to day in Jesus' name. I pray, AMEN!

**TODAY'S THOUGHT: Like Unforgiveness And Judgment, Mercy And Forgiveness Have A Boomerang Effect. They Will Come Back To Us!**

**My reflections for Today:** _____
_____
_____
_____
_____

# THIRD WEEK – WEDNESDAY FOCUS

## Spiritual Vitamin: Offended? Forgive and give up the resentment!

**SCRIPTURE: Luke 17:3-5 (AMP)**
*"Pay attention and always be on guard looking out for one another! If your brother sins and disregards God's precepts, solemnly warn him; and if he repents and changes, forgive him. ⁴ Even if he sins against you seven times a day, and returns to you seven times and says, 'I repent,' you must forgive him that is, give up resentment and consider the offense recalled and annulled."*

**SONG: "I MUST TELL JESUS" (Elisha A. Huffman)**

**PRAYER:** Lord, please help me! I need Your Holy Spirit to walk with me through these experiences so that I emerge **better**, not bitter. Please help me let go of negativity and resentment. I must hold on to Your Precepts and Power, in Jesus' name, AMEN!

**TODAY'S THOUGHT: My Heart Is Not Available For Bitterness And Resentment. I Walk In Forgiveness, And The Holy Spirit Occupies All Of My Heart.**

**My reflections for Today:**_____

_____

_____

_____

# THIRD WEEK – THURSDAY FOCUS

**Spiritual Vitamin: Jesus does <u>not</u> condemn! Jesus forgives!**

## SCRIPTURE: ST. JOHN 8:9-11(GNT)

*"When they heard this, they all left, one by one, the older ones first. Jesus was left alone, with the woman still standing there. He straightened up and said to her, "Where are they? Is there no one left to condemn you?" "No one, sir," she answered. "Well, then," Jesus said, "I do not condemn you either. Go, but do not sin again."*

## SONG: "YES, GOD IS REAL!" (Kenneth Morris)

**PRAYER**: Dear God, thank You so much for a clean slate! You have forgiven my sins and washed me in the Blood of Jesus Christ. Now, Lord, please help me to forgive myself and move on to live an abundant life. You said in Your Word that You do not condemn me, and I believe in that reality. Thank You, Father, for the freedom this knowledge brings to my life. I love You, Lord, and praise You in Jesus' name, AMEN!

**TODAY'S THOUGHT: It Is A Waste Of Time To Condemn What God Has Already Blessed!**

My reflections for Today: _____

_____

_____

_____

_____

# THIRD WEEK – FRIDAY FOCUS

**Spiritual Vitamin: God loved us first. Now He wants us to love Him and each other!**

## SCRIPTURE: 1 JOHN 4:7-11 (KJV)

*"Beloved, let us love one another: for love is of God; every one that loveth is born of God, and knoweth God. He that loveth not knoweth not God; for God is love. In this was manifested the love of God toward us, because that God sent his only begotten Son into the world, that we might live through him. Herein is love, not that we loved God, but that he loved us, and sent his Son to be the propitiation for our sins. Beloved, if God so loved us, we ought also to love one another."*

## SONG: "O, HOW I LOVE JESUS! (Isaac Watts and Frederick Whitehead)

**PRAYER:** Dear God, Your Word reveals love's ultimate example. Your Son, Jesus Christ, willingly laid down His life for me. I acknowledge that Jesus is knocking at my heart's door, motivating me to build a love relationship with Him and with others. Please forgive me for not being more alert to His prompting. Thank You for Your Presence and Love in my life. And, thank You for Jesus, the ultimate sacrifice made for our sins. It is His Name we pray in His name, AMEN!

**TODAY'S THOUGHT: I Choose To Love And Have An Intimate Relationship With God Above Everything Else!**

My reflections for Today: _____
_____
_____
_____
_____

# Third Week – Saturday Focus

**Spiritual Vitamin: Don't be troubled or afraid.
Pursue God's peace in all things"**

**SCRIPTURE: 1 PETER 3:9-11 (NIV)**
*"Do not repay evil with evil or insult with insult. On the contrary, repay evil with blessing because to this you were called so that you may inherit a blessing. [10] For, "Whoever would love life and see good days must keep their tongue from evil and their lips from deceitful speech.[11] They must turn from evil and do good; they must <u>seek peace and pursue it</u>."*

**SONG: "MASTER, THE TEMPEST IS RAGING (Mary A. Baker & Horatio H. Palmer)**

**PRAYER:** God of Peace, I am so thankful that you bring Peace that surpasses all understanding. Today, please allow us to experience the quietness and assurance of Your Peace. Keep us focused on pursuing and, running after Your Peace. Your Word reminds us that the children of God are peacemakers. Pour Your Peace upon us today and every day in Jesus' name, AMEN.

**TODAY'S THOUGHT: Jesus Said, "I Don't Give You The World's Peace, I Give You <u>My Peace</u>! "That Spells Victory For Us!**

**My reflections for Today:** _____
_____
_____
_____
_____

MY SINCERE COMMITMENT:

I WILL <u>NOT</u> ALLOW THE ADVERSARY
TO STEAL MY POSITION AS A CHOSEN
VESSEL OF GOD! I HAVE BEEN
WASHED IN THE BLOOD OF THE LAMB!
SATAN HAS <u>NOT</u> HAD THIS PRIVILEGE
AND NEVER WILL!

# FOURTH SUNDAY IN LENT - WEEKLY MEDITATION

---

## Urgent Call! Seek God While He May Be Found!

**SCRIPTURE: ISAIAH 55:6-7 (NLT)** *"Seek the Lord while you can find him. Call on him now while he is near. Let the wicked change their ways and banish the very thought of doing wrong. Let them turn to the Lord that he may have mercy on them. Yes, turn to our God, for he will forgive generously."*

**PSALM 32:6-7 (NIV)** *"Therefore let all the faithful pray to you while you may be found; surely the rising of the mighty waters will not reach them. You are my hiding place; you will protect me from trouble and surround me with songs of deliverance."*

The COVID-19 pandemic has not only been a traumatic experience for all of us, but its growing impact is very troubling. With more than 800,000 persons succumbing to the ravages of COVID, the world, and especially the United States, waited with bated breath for news of vaccines and cures. Many have already received vaccines, and booster shots, and drugs are being tested to secure a successful treatment for the disease. Unfortunately, while many apply individual safeguards, as directed by the CDC, many continue to ignore the precautions. The result is that variants are developing quickly, and we appear to be going in circles.

Is it possible that God is pressing a reset button in preparation for a new thing? Think about it. When my computer or phone malfunctions, I often find shutting down entirely and re-starting the process usually corrects what's wrong. May I suggest business and life as we knew them before the pandemic began will not be the same again? Many have accepted that and are looking for a "new normal." God has a plan that will deliver us all and prepare us for the second coming of Christ.

In His Word, God repeatedly warns us about time. He loves us very much and is not willing for anyone to perish but all of us should have an opportunity for reconciliation. When we reflect on these scripture verses, we cannot help but see the loving Savior beckoning us. God reminds us that we don't have as much time as we think we have. Most of all, He admonishes us to use our time wisely.

God desires we seek Him for direction, for answers, for healing, for every facet of our lives. However, when we lean to our understanding and attempt to establish our "new normal" without Him, we again place ourselves at the beginning of the process cycle. The Word of God promises "if my people, who are called by my name, will humble themselves and pray and seek my face and turn from their wicked ways, then I will hear from heaven, and I will forgive their sin and will heal their land." This week, let's examine whether we have humbled ourselves to pray, seek His face, or turned from our wicked ways. Our individual and corporate spiritual assessment may find breaches in our humility, prayer lives, and determination to seek HIS FACE!

The scriptures listed above urge us to SEEK GOD NOW! They confirm God is willing to forgive if we take the time to seek Him and change our ways. God has promised we will be delivered when we are obedient to this invitation.

**PRAYER:** Father, thank You so much for Your patience with Your children. Your love for us is unconditional. And, we hear Your voice beckoning us to seek more of You. Please help us to do that in Spirit and in truth. Our hearts thank you for this great invitation, AMEN!

**TODAY'S THOUGHT: Don't Procrastinate! Seek God Now! He Is Our Hiding Place And Our Deliverer!**

# FOURTH WEEK

## SONG – O THOU, IN WHOSE PRESENCE (Joseph Swain)

O Thou, in Whose presence my soul takes delight
On Whom in affliction, I call
My comfort by day, and my song in the night
My hope, my salvation, my all

Where dost thou, dear Shepherd resort with thy sheep
To feed them in pastures of love?
Say, why in the valley of death should I weep
Or alone in this wilderness rove?

Oh, why should I wander, an alien from Thee
Or cry in the desert for bread?
Thy foes will rejoice when my sorrows they see
And smile at the tears I have shed

He looks, and ten thousands of angels rejoice
And myriads wait for His Word
He speaks and eternity, filled with His voice
Re-echoes the praise of the Lord

Dear Shepherd, I hear and will follow Thy call
I know the sweet sound of Thy voice
Restore and defend me, for Thou art my all
And in Thee, I will ever rejoice.

**My reflections for Today:** _____

_____

_____

_____

# Fourth Week – Monday Focus

**Spiritual Vitamin: Godly humility attracts God's attention!**

## SCRIPTURE: 2 CHRONICLES 34:27 (KJV)

*"Because thine heart was tender, and thou didst humble thyself before God, when thou heardest his words against this place, and against the inhabitants thereof, and humblest thyself before me, and didst rend thy clothes, and weep before me; I have even heard thee also, saith the Lord."*

## SONG: "I NEED THEE EVERY HOUR" (Annie Hawks and Robert Lowry)

**PRAYER:** Dear God, we bow before you, acknowledging we are dependent on You for everything. Please forgive us for ever thinking we could move or exist without You. We need You, Lord! Bind selfishness, self-centeredness, and anything that causes pride to increase in us. We know that wisdom is born from humility and the fear of the Lord. Shape us for Your Glory in Jesus' name, AMEN!

**TODAY'S THOUGHT: Stay Humble And Stay In Touch With God!**

My reflections for Today:_____

_____

_____

_____

_____

# Fourth Week – Tuesday Focus

**Spiritual Vitamin: Watch and be sober! Don't Stop Praying!**

## SCRIPTURE: 1 THESSALONIANS 5:16-23 (KJV)

*"Rejoice evermore. Pray without ceasing. In everything give thanks: for this is the will of God in Christ Jesus concerning you. Quench not the Spirit. Despise not prophesyings. Prove all things; hold fast that which is good. Abstain from all appearance of evil. And the very God of peace sanctify you wholly, and I pray God your whole spirit and soul and body be preserved blameless unto the coming of our Lord Jesus Christ."*

## SONG: "SWEET HOUR OF PRAYER" (William Walford and William P. Bradbury)

**PRAYER:** Holy God, we recognize Your rulership in our lives, and we are grateful. Thank You for your plans for us. You have been kind and faithful to our families, churches, and communities. However, I confess that we sometimes fell asleep on the prayer watch. Please forgive us and help us be sober, to watch and pray at all times. Father, call us into a deeper, more intimate prayer life and a closer relationship with You, in Jesus' name, AMEN.

## TODAY'S THOUGHT: Jesus Is One Prayer Away! Just Whisper A Prayer!

**My reflections for Today:**_____ ˒

_____

_____

_____

_____

# FOURTH WEEK – WEDNESDAY FOCUS

**Spiritual Vitamin: The wilderness is a dry, deserted, and desolate place. Make sure God is your leader!**

## SCRIPTURE: PSALM 42:1-2 (NIV)

*"As the deer pants for streams of water, so my soul pants for you, my God. My soul thirsts for God, for the living God. When can I go and meet with God?"*

## SONG: "O, THOU IN WHOSE PRESENCE, MY SOUL TAKES DELIGHT" (Joseph Swain)

**PRAYER:** Lord, how we need you! We are very thirsty for Your Presence, for Your touch, for Your anointing. We are chasing after You today. Please hear our prayer. Our minds and souls are tired. The enemy oppresses us, yet we know You are able! Father, please breathe on every component of our lives. Change us amid this wilderness experience, and kindle renewed spiritual, emotional, physical, intellectual, and economic power and revitalization within us in the precious name of Jesus we pray, AMEN.

**TODAY'S THOUGHT: Chase After God! We Need Him To Have Victory In This Wilderness!**

**My reflections for Today:** _____

_____

_____

_____

_____

# Fourth Week – Thursday Focus

**Spiritual Vitamin: Repentance requires
turning our backs on all wrong!**

## SCRIPTURE: ACTS 26:16-18 (KJV)

*"But rise, and stand upon thy feet: for I have appeared unto thee for this purpose, to make thee a minister and a witness both of these things which thou hast seen, and of those things in the which I will appear unto thee; Delivering thee from the people, and from the Gentiles, unto whom now I send thee, To open their eyes, and to turn them from darkness to light, and from the power of Satan unto God, that they may receive forgiveness of sins, and inheritance among them which are sanctified by faith that is in me."*

## SONG: "ALL TO JESUS, I SURRENDER" (Judson Vandeventer and Winfield Weeden)

**PRAYER:** Lord of Heaven, we praise Your Holy Name! Father, thank you for Jesus, our Savior. He has provided us with a way of being reconciled with You. Thank you, Jesus! We repent and turn away from everything in our lives that displeases You. We want our lives to bring glory to Your name. So, please help us make Christ-like decisions and choices. Our desire is to be accepted and approved by You, Lord, not by people. Fill us with Your Presence and Your Word so we can help others turn away from sin before it is eternally too late. Make us effective instruments in Your hands, in Jesus' name, AMEN!

**TODAY'S THOUGHT: Jesus Delivered Us From People And Turned Our Darkness Into Light! We Accept His Charge To Help Others Turn From Darkness To Light!**

**My reflections for Today:**_____

_____

_____

_____

_____

# FOURTH WEEK – FRIDAY FOCUS

**Spiritual Vitamin: God always has you covered
especially when you are battle-weary.
BE ENCOURAGED!**

## SCRIPTURE: ISAIAH 60:1-2 (NIV)

*"Arise, shine, for your light has come, and the glory of the Lord rises upon you. See, darkness covers the earth, and thick darkness is over the peoples, but the Lord rises upon you, and His glory appears over you."*

## SONG: "WHEN I ROSE THIS MORNING, I DIDN'T HAVE NO DOUBT" (Carlton Reese)

**PRAYER:** Thank you, Lord, for another day! We praise and thank You for the gift of life. You have watched over and kept us safe from harm and danger. Our hearts are grateful for Your grace and mercy. Yet, father, darkness, sickness, evil, and plague are all around us. We praise You because of Jesus, Your light is <u>expressly in, over, and around us</u>. Our faith is strengthened when we remember Your investment in us! Thank you, Jesus! Today, please bathe us in Your Presence so Jesus can be clearly seen in us. It is in Jesus' name we pray, AMEN.

**TODAY'S THOUGHT: Don't Be Discouraged! God's Got Your Back!**

My reflections for Today:_____

_____

_____

_____

_____

# FOURTH WEEK – SATURDAY FOCUS

## SPIRITUAL VITAMIN: News Bulletin! We Are In A Spiritual War! Are You Prepared?

## SCRIPTURE: EPHESIANS 6:10-17 (TLB)

*"Last of all, I want to remind you that your strength must come from the Lord's mighty power within you. Put on all of God's armor so that you will be able to stand safe against all strategies and tricks of Satan. For we are not fighting against people made of flesh and blood, but against persons without bodies—the evil rulers of the unseen world, those mighty satanic beings and great evil princes of darkness who rule this world; and against huge numbers of wicked spirits in the spirit world. So use every piece of God's armor to resist the enemy whenever he attacks, and when it is all over, you will still be standing up. But to do this, you will need the strong belt of truth and the breastplate of God's approval. Wear shoes that are able to speed you on as you preach the Good News of peace with God. In every battle, you will need faith as your shield to stop the fiery arrows aimed at you by Satan. And you will need the helmet of salvation and the sword of the Spirit—which is the Word of God."*

## SONG: "GOD NEVER FAILS" (George Jordan & Harold Smith)

God never fails. God never fails. He abides with me.
He gives me victory
No, God never fails. Just keep the faith and never
cease to pray
Just walk upright; call Him noon, day or night.
He'll be there. He'll be there. There's no need to worry,
For God never fails!'

**PRAYER:** Lord God Sabaoth, God of the Angel Armies, we honor You today. You are a warrior God, and You are teaching us to be spiritually prepared to triumph over the adversary. You are the Lord of Hosts! Help us study Your battle plan and allow the Holy Spirit to train us to be effective warriors. Jesus, we need Your battle gear, Your power, and strength to keep the faith. Please give us a praying spirit to continuously connect to Your trustworthy source of discernment and direction. Forgive us for attempting to engage in spiritual battles without the appropriate spiritual gear. Please help us trade in our tattered clothing and weapons for the spiritual armor You have available for Your "new people." We ask this in Jesus' name, AMEN.

**TODAY'S THOUGHT: The World Is A Battleground! Warrior, Put Your War Clothes On And Stay Battle-Ready!**

**My reflections for Today:** _____

_____

_____

_____

_____

MY SINCERE COMMITMENT:

I WILL <u>NOT</u> ALLOW THE ADVERSARY
TO STEAL MY POSITION AS A CHOSEN
VESSEL OF GOD! I HAVE BEEN
WASHED IN THE BLOOD OF THE LAMB!
SATAN HAS <u>NOT</u> HAD THIS PRIVILEGE
AND NEVER WILL!

# FIFTH SUNDAY IN LENT
# WEEKLY MEDITATION

---

## God's People Can No Longer Be Timid!
## We Are Armed And Dangerous To Satan's
## Kingdom, And He Knows It!

### SCRIPTURE: ROMANS 1:16-17 (KJV)

*"For I am not ashamed of the gospel of Christ: for it is the power of God unto salvation to every one that believeth; to the Jew first, and also to the Greek. For therein is the righteousness of God revealed from faith to faith: as it is written, The just shall live by faith."*

Beloved, we have been under relentless attack by the adversary. Unfortunately, many of us have attempted to get through these attacks without fortifying ourselves with protection and the proper weapons specifically designed for the battle. We, therefore, become unaware of the enemy's activities and fall prey to his devious ways. Sometimes, we decline from doing the right thing because we want to relieve the adversary's pressure on us. We simply cave in or give up! For example, have you ever been in the presence of wrongdoing and neglected to speak up for fear you might be criticized or ostracized by your peers? Sure, all of us have at some time!

Do we realize the power available to us when we take a stand for the Gospel of Jesus Christ? Just as Paul did, we need to declare our loyalty and faith in Jesus Christ and declare by our witness and behavior that: "I am not ashamed of the Gospel of Jesus Christ!" Let's send a clear and powerful faith message to the world! Our regular declaration of loyalty is what grows us from faith to faith!

As we study the Word of God, we find those who believed in God's Power and were loyal to His Word had extraordinary victorious experiences! In this season, I believe God is looking for His children to change their approach. So far, our plan for spiritual warfare has been to react. I believe God wants us to be in condition and a position to be proactive, and to advance on the adversary! That is, God gives us the power and anointing to discern an attack long before it happens. In this season, God wants us to listen to the Holy Spirit and be spiritually ready and able to move at a moment's notice to do His bidding.

So, how do we prepare to be warriors? It is a simple process. First, let's submit ourselves to God daily, moment by moment. Spend time in prayer and fellowship with Him. Then, let's study and be obedient to the Word of God. We must be confident in what we believe and stand firmly on it, no matter what. In addition, let's remember we are human. Jesus is the only one who is perfect; we are not! But we are moving toward perfection! Seek God's Power and the Holy Spirit to direct every facet of our lives. Let Him fill and re-fill us so that we are consistently using His Power, not our own. Remember, Jesus is holding us and is interceding for us in Heaven's Throneroom! Thank You, Jesus! Finally, let's focus on and trust in God's plan for our victory, not on the battle itself. The battle belongs to God! Remember Psalm 125:1 (NIV) says, "Those who trust in the Lord are like Mount Zion, which cannot be shaken but endures forever."

So, don't be ashamed of the Gospel of Jesus Christ. It gives us the power to overcome!

**PRAYER**: Dear God, our Father, how wonderful You are! We worship and honor You. We thank You for Jesus, who made it possible for us to be reconciled with You. What a wonderful Savior He is! Thank You for the love and protection You provide for us. Lord, we desire to be stalwart soldiers of the cross. We want to be fit for battle. Will You please teach us how to be conditioned to Your battle strategies and plans? We release our desires and "things as usual" to passionately embrace your New Season for the Kingdom. Thank You for allowing us to prepare for Your second coming, in Jesus' name, AMEN.

**TODAY'S THOUGHT: Jesus rescued us from everlasting death. We will trust Him forever and never be ashamed to tell the Good News to all people!**

# FIFTH WEEK IN LENT

## SONG: "STAND UP, STAND UP FOR JESUS" (George Duffield and George J. Webb)

Stand up, stand up for Jesus, Ye soldiers of the cross;
Lift high his royal banner. It must not suffer loss.
From victory unto victory His army shall He lead,
Till every foe is vanquished, And Christ is Lord indeed.

Stand up, stand up for Jesus, The trumpet call obey
Forth to the mighty conflict In this His glorious day
Ye that are men now serve Him Against unnumbered foe
Let courage rise with danger And strength to strength
oppose,

Stand up, stand up for Jesus, Stand in his strength alone;
The arm of flesh will fail you. Ye dare not trust your own.
Put on the gospel armor. Each piece put on with prayer;
Where duty calls or danger, Be never wanting there.

Stand up, stand up for Jesus, The strife will not be long;
This day the noise of battle, The next the victor's song.
To him that overcometh A crown of life shall be;
They, with the King of Glory, Shall reign eternally.

**My reflections for Today:** _____

_____

_____

_____

_____

# Fifth Week – Monday Focus

**Spiritual Vitamin: This is an urgent call for every Christian to grow up spiritually!**

## SCRIPTURE: HEBREWS 5:11-14 (NLT)

*"There is much more we would like to say about this, but it is difficult to explain, especially since you are spiritually dull and don't seem to listen. You have been believers so long now that you ought to be teaching others. Instead, you need someone to teach you again the basic things about God's Word. You are like babies who need milk and cannot eat solid food. For someone who lives on milk is still an infant and doesn't know how to do what is right. Solid food is for those who are mature, who through training have the skill to recognize the difference between right and wrong."*

## SONG: "I AM WEAK, AND I NEED THY STRENGTH" (Doris Akers)

I am weak, and I need Thy strength and power to help me over my weakest hour;
Let me through the darkness Thy face to see, Lead me O Lord, lead me.

Help me tread in the paths of righteousness; Be my aid when Satan and sin oppress;
I am putting all my trust in Thee, Lead me O Lord, lead me

Chorus: Lead me, guide me along the way; for if You lead me, I cannot stray;
Lord, let me walk each day with Thee, Lead me, O Lord, lead me.

**PRAYER:** Dear Heavenly Father, I am incredibly thankful that when I am at my lowest ebb, Jesus is interceding for me. How I bless You for Jesus, my Savior! I desire to be stronger, better. bolder, and more mature spiritually. Please forgive me for not consuming adequate spiritual food. Lord, please help me grow and operate in Your wisdom so that I can recognize and do Your will. I desire a more intimate relationship with You, Father. I need Your Presence, Your precious Word, Your Power and Your Love. Take away those things that keep me from spending time with You. Help me focus on growing into a strong tree of righteousness in Jesus' name I pray, AMEN.

**TODAY'S THOUGHT: We Cannot Afford To Remain Immature Christians. God Has Much Work For Us To Do.**

**My reflections for Today:**_____

_____

_____

_____

_____

# FIFTH WEEK – TUESDAY FOCUS

**Spiritual Vitamin: Forget what we used to do! God has set our course. It's a highway through the wilderness! Get ready!**

## SCRIPTURE: ISAIAH 43:18-21 (NLT)

*"But forget all that— it is nothing compared to what I am going to do. For I am about to do something new. See, I have already begun! Do you not see it? I will make a pathway through the wilderness. I will create rivers in the dry wasteland. The wild animals in the fields will thank me, the jackals and owls, too, for giving them water in the desert. Yes, I will make rivers in the dry wasteland so my chosen people can be refreshed. I have made Israel for myself, and they will someday honor me before the whole world."*

## SONG: "I WILL DO A NEW THING IN YOU" (Derek Dunn)

"I will do a new thing in you; I will do a new thing in you;
Whatever you ask for, whatever you pray for,
Nothing shall be denied," saith the Lord; saith the Lord!

**PRAYER:** Heavenly Father, Creator of the universe, Giver and Preserver of life, we are grateful for Your unfailing love and mercy. We acknowledge with joy Your wisdom and power. We see Your Hand at work in our world and thank You for always shepherding Your children. How grateful we are for Your faithfulness to us! We discern Your plan to move us in a new direction with sharpened tools and more significant influence. Thank You, Lord, for providing a highway through the wilderness! Father, we see the signs of the return of the Lord Jesus Christ, and we want to join You in ministering love to the world in this season. Lord, please do a new thing in us. Prepare us to receive Your miraculous agenda. Bend us, make us flexible and open to receive direction from You as we await the second coming of the Lord Jesus Christ. Help us hear You and obey, in the precious name of Jesus, our Lord, AMEN.

**TODAY'S THOUGHT: Let's Stop Trying To Establish <u>A New Normal</u>. Let's Flow With God! He Already Has A Plan For His People!**

**My reflections for Today:**_____

_____

_____

_____

_____

# FIFTH WEEK – WEDNESDAY FOCUS

**Spiritual Vitamin: Let's make sure we don't
<u>waste the New Wine</u> by not being in condition
to receive what God has in store for us!**

## SCRIPTURE: MATTHEW 9:16-17 (NLT)

*"Besides, who would patch old clothing with new cloth? For the new patch would shrink and rip away from the old cloth, leaving an even bigger tear than before. "And no one puts new wine into old wineskins. For the old skins would burst from the pressure, spilling the wine and ruining the skins. New wine is stored in new wineskins so that both are preserved."*

## SONG: "WHAT A WONDERFUL CHANGE IN MY LIFE – SINCE JESUS CAME INTO MY HEART" (Rufus McDaniel, Charles Gabriel)

**PRAYER:** Dear God, thank You for changing our lives, for causing us to look at ourselves through the lens of Your dear Son, Jesus, the Christ. Please forgive us for trying to hold on to old ways, old thoughts, old attitudes, and old relationships that do not comport with Your Word. Father God, we open ourselves to You for constant renewal, restoration, and strength. You are the Lord of our lives! Please do with us as You see fit so we can be effective instruments in Your Hands. Thank You for loving us to the degree You invested Your Son's life for us so we might live! We offer this prayer in Jesus' name, AMEN.

**TODAY'S THOUGHT: We Are New Vessels Consumed With Hope, Steadfast And Sure!**

**My reflections for Today:**_____

_____

_____

_____

_____

# Fifth Week – Thursday Focus

**Spiritual Vitamin: God's people must be spiritually awake and vibrant. We must not be afraid to leave old things behind to embrace what is new and relevant.**

## SCRIPTURE: 2 CORINTHIANS 5:16:17 (AMP)

*"So from now on, we regard no one from a human point of view [according to worldly standards and values]. Though we have known Christ from a human point of view, now we no longer know Him in this way. Therefore, if anyone is in Christ [that is, grafted in, joined to Him by faith in Him as Savior], he is a new creature [reborn and renewed by the Holy Spirit]; the old things [the previous moral and spiritual condition] have passed away. Behold, new things have come [because spiritual awakening brings a new life]."*

## SONG: "I GOT A NEW NAME OVER IN ZION" (Traditional Negro Spiritual)

**PRAYER:** Lord of Heaven, we bless You today for a new start. You have made us a new creation in Christ Jesus and written our names in the Lamb's Book of Life. Praise Your Holy Name! Pour upon us Your Holy Spirit, the Teacher, the Enabler, so we may receive Your vision and instructions. Your joy is filling us and giving us strength. Your might provides us the power to walk where we have never been before. Your Spirit teaches us wisdom and understanding of Your Word and Your plan for our lives. Thank You, Father. Please strengthen us to be obedient. Help us never to judge others, but to do all things in love so that we bring glory and honor to You, in Jesus' name, AMEN.

**TODAY'S THOUGHT: In Christ, We Are A New Creation With A New Focus!**

**My reflections for Today:** _____

_____

_____

_____

# Fifth Week – Friday Focus

**Spiritual Vitamin: When Things Get Tough, Don't Worry! God's Glory Will Be Revealed In Us After A While!**

## SCRIPTURE: ROMANS 8:14-18 (GNT)

*"Those who are led by God's Spirit are God's children. For the Spirit that God has given you does not make you slaves and cause you to be afraid; instead, the Spirit makes you God's children, and by the Spirit's power, we cry out to God, "Father! my Father!" God's Spirit joins himself to our spirits to declare that we are God's children. Since we are his children, we will possess the blessings he keeps for his people, and we will also possess with Christ what God has kept for him; for if we share Christ's suffering, we will also share his glory. I consider that what we suffer at this present time cannot be compared at all with the glory that is going to be revealed to us."*

## SONG: THE CENTER OF MY JOY (Richard Smallwood)

When I've lost my direction, You're the <u>compass</u> for my way.
You're the fire and <u>light</u> when <u>nights</u> are long and cold.
In sadness, You are the laughter that <u>shatters</u> all my fears.
When I'm all alone, Your hand is <u>there</u> to hold,

You are why I find <u>pleasure</u> in the <u>simple</u> things in life
You're the <u>music</u> in the <u>meadows</u> and the streams
The <u>voices</u> of the children, my family, and my home
You're the <u>source</u> and <u>finish</u> of my <u>highest</u> dreams,

Chorus: Jesus, You're the <u>center</u> of my joy. All that's
good and <u>perfect</u> comes from you
You're the <u>heart</u> of my contentment, hope for all I do.
Jesus, you're the <u>center</u> of my joy.

**PRAYER:** Heavenly Father, we thank You for another day. Praise
Your name for mercy and grace has walked with us, and we are
grateful. We honor You, Abba Father, for redeeming us to Yourself
and making us joint-heirs with Your Son, Jesus. We know He suffered
many things, and we, too, must suffer so Your Glory can be seen in
us. We know You are with us, and we pledge our loyalty and trust
to You. We believe in Your Word. We trust Your Presence; we have
proven Your Power! Thank you, Lord, for the hope and the peace
that is within us. We praise You in Jesus' name, AMEN.

**TODAY'S THOUGHT: As Christians, We Gratefully Share
In Christ's Suffering. We Are Joint-Heirs With Christ! Our
Suffering Cannot Be Compared To The Glory That Is To Come!**

**My reflections for Today:**_____
_____
_____
_____
_____

# FIFTH WEEK – SATURDAY FOCUS

**Spiritual Vitamin: Nothing and no-one can harm us when we trust and live by the promises of God."**

## SCRIPTURE: 2 Timothy 2:10-13 (TLB)

*"I am more than willing to suffer if that will bring salvation and eternal glory in Christ Jesus to those God has chosen. I am comforted by this truth, that when we suffer and die for Christ it only means that we will begin living with him in heaven. And if we think that our present service for him is hard, just remember that someday we are going to sit with him and rule with him. But if we give up when we suffer, and turn against Christ, then he must turn against us. Even when we are too weak to have any faith left, he remains faithful to us and will help us, for he cannot disown us who are part of himself, and he will always carry out his promises to us."*

## SONG; "Standing on the Promises of Christ my King" (R. Kelso Carter)

**PRAYER:** Dear Heavenly Father, Your Word declares that You always do exactly what You promise. Thank you for your faithful promises. When we become tired and afraid, Your faithful covenant renews us and keeps us focused on Your Will. By Your living Word, we prevail in every situation. Praise Your Holy Name! We honor You for Your commitment to us and pray for the release of additional strength and power in Jesus' name, AMEN.

**TODAY'S THOUGHT: We Overcome The World Daily By Standing On The Promises Of God!**

**Thoughts for Today:**_____

_____

_____

_____

_____

MY SINCERE COMMITMENT:

I WILL <u>NOT</u> ALLOW THE ADVERSARY
TO STEAL MY POSITION AS A CHOSEN
VESSEL OF GOD!  I HAVE BEEN
WASHED IN THE BLOOD OF THE LAMB!
SATAN HAS <u>NOT</u> HAD THIS PRIVILEGE
AND NEVER WILL!

# SIXTH SUNDAY IN LENT – (PALM SUNDAY) WEEKLY MEDITATION

---

## We Will Not Stop Praising Our God!
## That's What We Were Created To Do!

### SCRIPTURE: LUKE 19:32-40 (NIV)

*"Those who were sent ahead went and found it just as he had told them. As they were untying the colt, its owners asked them, "Why are you untying the colt?" They replied, "The Lord needs it." They brought it to Jesus, threw their cloaks on the colt, and put Jesus on it. As he went along, people spread their cloaks on the road. When he came near the place where the road goes down the Mount of Olives, the whole crowd of disciples began joyfully to praise God in loud voices for all the miracles they had seen: "Blessed is the king who comes in the name of the Lord! "Peace in heaven and glory in the highest!" Some of the Pharisees in the crowd said to Jesus, "Teacher, rebuke your disciples!" "I tell you," he replied, "if they keep quiet, the stones will cry out."*

Why do we sometimes allow others to intimidate us when praising our God? Modern-day Scribes and Pharisees are simply horrified when we make a joyful noise to our God. So we ignore them. Instead, we follow Biblical instructions and respond to the presence of a Holy God who loves us and has been faithful to us. We give honor where honor is due! Revelation 4:11 reminds us that we are created for God's pleasure. We are here to praise and honor Him; that is our function.

On Jesus' triumphant entry into Jerusalem, this was the scenario. He entered the city, riding on a donkey, and the people, remembering all His miracles and teaching, began to proclaim Him as King! They threw palm branches and their cloaks in the street. They honored Him and declared Him King of the Jews! In fact, the people blessed Him for coming in the name of the Lord. They praised Him so much the Pharisees asked Jesus to stop the crowd from giving him praise. Jesus told them if the crowd stops praising me, the rocks will take up where they left off.

The Word of God is replete with instructions for God's people to be generous in praising God. The psalmist David encourages us to praise God with every instrument available, everywhere we are. He even exhorts us to "lift our hands in the sanctuary" when nothing particular is planned and just worship God for who He is. In addition, consider all God has done for us. John 3:16 declares God so loved the world that He gave His only begotten Son, that whosoever believes in Him should not perish but shall have everlasting life – that's a gift! Praise God for Jesus!

## SONG: PRAISE HIM, HE'S WORTHY TO BE PRAISED (Donnie Harper)

**PRAYER:** Heavenly Father, we praise and honor You for the marvelous gift of Your dear Son, Jesus Christ. You called Him Jesus and assigned Him the ministry of bringing us into reconciliation with You. Thank You, Jesus, for your willingness to be the propitiation for our sins. We love You, Lord, and we worship and praise You! No rocks will cry out in our place. No one will keep us from celebrating and extolling You for real! You are the very breath we breathe, and You have given us Your authority! So, we bind intimidation and the spirit of fear in the name of Jesus. We surrender ourselves to the spirit of worship and freedom and pray that our families, churches, and communities will feel the impact of true worship of God in the name of Jesus our Lord and Master, AMEN.

**TODAY'S THOUGHT: When We Worship And Glorify God, It Makes God Happy And Offends The Adverary!**

**My reflections for Today:**_____

_____

_____

_____

_____

# HOLY WEEK – MONDAY FOCUS

### Spiritual Vitamin: Jesus Is The Light Of The World, And He Is Inside Us…Come On, Shine!

## SCRIPTURE: JOHN 12;35-36 (KJV)

*"Then Jesus said unto them, Yet a little while is the light with you. Walk while ye have the light, lest darkness come upon you: for he that walketh in darkness knoweth not whither he goeth. While ye have light, believe in the light, that ye may be the children of light. These things spake Jesus, and departed, and did hide himself from them."*

## SONG: "WALK IN THE LIGHT" (J. V. Combs)

> We'll walk in the light, beautiful light,
> Come where the dew-drops of mercy are bright;
> Shine all around us by day and by night, Jesus, the
> Light of the world.

**PRAYER:** Dear God, thank You for another day and for your mercy and grace. The world has become very dark, and life is difficult right now. Yet, we praise and thank you for the light we find in Jesus Christ. We cherish the light He brings to this world. Help us reflect the light of Jesus and represent Him well as we go about our daily lives. We discern the signs of the times. Please help us make good use of our time before Your return in Jesus' name, AMEN.

**TODAY'S THOUGHT: We Will Light Up The World With God's Loving Presence!**

**My reflections for Today:**_____

_____

_____

# Holy Week – Tuesday Focus

**Spiritual vitamin: God uses the simple things of life to accomplish complicated agendas.**

## SCRIPTURE: 1 CORINTHIANS 1:26-29 (TLB)

*"Notice among yourselves, dear brothers, that few of you who follow Christ have big names or power or wealth. Instead, God has deliberately chosen to use ideas the world considers foolish and of little worth in order to shame those people considered by the world as wise and great. He has chosen a plan despised by the world, counted as nothing at all, and used it to bring down to nothing those the world considers great, so that no one anywhere can ever brag in the presence of God."*

## SONG: "I WILL TRUST IN THE LORD" (Isaac Watts)

**PRAYER:** Heavenly Father, Your wisdom and attention to detail are incredible. Your Word declares that you confound the wise by using the simple things of life to accomplish Your agendas. Praise Your Holy and Righteous Name! We appreciate every blessing, every deliverance, and everything You have done to ensure that we can have a love relationship with You. You did it simply, and we reverence Your plans. Now, please help us trust You and remain humble so that You can use us for Your glory. We pray in Jesus' name, AMEN.

**TODAY'S THOUGHT: The World Cannot Discern Nor Understand The Things Of God!**

**My reflections for Today:**_____

_____

_____

_____

_____

# Holy Week – Wednesday Focus

### Spiritual Vitamin: The world is watching – let go of everything that hinders progress!

**SCRIPTURE: HEBREWS 12:1-2 (NLT)**
*"Therefore, since we are surrounded by such a huge crowd of witnesses to the life of faith, let us strip off every weight that slows us down, especially the sin that so easily trips us up. And let us run with endurance the race God has set before us. We do this by keeping our eyes on Jesus, the champion who initiates and perfects our faith. Because of the joy awaiting him, he endured the cross, disregarding its shame. Now he is seated in the place of honor beside God's throne."*

**SONG: "HAVE THINE OWN WAY LORD" (Adelaide Pollard)**

**PRAYER:** O Heavenly Father, thank You for calling us from a world of darkness into Your marvelous light. We esteem Your Presence and the gifts You have bestowed on us. You have loaded us with blessings daily. Yet, we have also been encumbered with care as we deal with the challenges of COVID 19, political recklessness, economic challenges, and family difficulties. Dear Lord, please help us to lay aside every weight that keeps us from running the race that is before us. We are a new people, waiting to journey in a new direction with You. Kindly help us keep our eyes on Jesus, our champion and our King. It is in His name that we place these petitions, AMEN.

**TODAY'S THOUGHT: Let It Be Known That Our Eyes And Our Faith Are Focused On Jesus!**

My reflections for Today:_____
_____
_____

# Holy Week – Maundy Thursday Focus

### Spiritual Vitamin: We Know Jesus! He Lives In Us And Will Never Leave Nor Forsake Us!

## SCRIPTURE: JOHN 14:15-20 (NIV)

*"If you love me, keep my commands. And I will ask the Father, and he will give you another advocate to help you and be with you forever—the Spirit of truth. The world cannot accept Him because it neither sees him nor knows him. But you know him, for he lives with you and will be[c] in you. I will not leave you as orphans; I will come to you. Before long, the world will not see me anymore, but you will see me. Because I live, you also will live. On that day, you will realize that I am in my Father, and you are in me, and I am in you."*

## SONG: "WHEN WE WALK WITH THE LORD (TRUST AND OBEY) (John Sammis, Daniel Towner)

**PRAYER:** Dear God, thank You for the Holy Spirit who has taken up residence in us. He is our guide, teacher, agent of discernment, and company keeper. You have blessed us tremendously with His presence. Lord, please fill us again with Your Spirit. May we experience a double portion of Your presence and Your power during this season. We need You, Lord. We just cannot make it without You. So, as we spend time with you, Father, fill us with Your Holy Spirit. We wait for Your outpouring and pray that You will magnify Yourself in us this day, in Jesus' name, AMEN.

## TODAY'S THOUGHT: We Submit Ourselves To You, God. Fill Us With Your Holy Spirit Until We Overflow!

**My reflections for Today:** _____

_____

_____

_____

# Good Friday Focus

**SPIRITUAL VITAMIN: We Remember The Passion Of The Lord Jesus Christ. He Who Knew No Sin Became The Sacrificial Lamb For The Sins Of Humanity**

**SCRIPTURES: JESUS SPEAKS FROM THE CROSS- (KJV)**

THE WORD OF FORGIVENESS
"FATHER, FORGIVE THEM FOR THEY
KNOW NOT WHAT THEY DO."
LUKE 23:34

THE WORD OF SALVATION
"TODAY SHALT THOU BE WITH ME IN PARADISE"
LUKE 23:43

THE WORD OF ADOPTION
"WOMAN, BEHOLD THY SON. SON,
BEHOLD THY MOTHER."
JOHN 19:26

THE WORD OF ABANDONMENT
"MY GOD, MY GOD, WHY HAS THOU FORSAKEN ME?"
MATTHEW 27:46

THE WORD OF SUFFERING
"I THIRST"
JOHN 19:28

THE WORD OF COMPLETION
"IT IS FINISHED"
JOHN 19:30

## THE WORD OF VICTORY
## "FATHER, INTO THY HANDS I COMMEND MY SPIRIT"
## LUKE 23:46

**SONG: Jesus Keep Me Near the Cross (Fanny Crosby, William Doane)**

**PRAYER:** Dear Heavenly Father, how we thank You today for Jesus, Your Son, and the finished work of redemption on Calvary's Cross. Jesus experienced shame, pain and was beaten to ensure that our sins would be covered. Lord, when we consider the suffering He endured, we are more convinced than ever of our need to repent and live a life that pleases You. So, we surrender our lives to You all over again. Thank You, Father, for allowing Your Dear Son to be the sacrificial lamb for our sins. Your Word tells us Jesus was wounded for our transgressions, bruised for our iniquities, the chastisement of our peace is upon Him, and with His stripes, we are healed! Thank You, Lord, for Calvary! We also praise Your name because we know that Resurrection Day is coming! Thank You, Jesus! Just as you raised Jesus on Resurrection Day, help us to live so we can be ready when Jesus returns to carry us home. We offer this prayer of thanksgiving and surrender in His Name, AMEN.

**TODAY'S THOUGHT: Jesus Surrendered His Life For You At Calvary! He Did Not Have To Do it, He Could Have Called On Angels From Glory To Rescue Him, But He Finished His Divine Assignment. So, We Now Have An Advocate With God In The Person Of Jesus Christ! How Will You Respond? Resurrection Day Is Coming.**

**My reflections for Today:** _____

_____

_____

_____

_____

MY SINCERE COMMITMENT:

I WILL <u>NOT</u> ALLOW THE ADVERSARY
TO STEAL MY POSITION AS A CHOSEN
VESSEL OF GOD!  I HAVE BEEN
WASHED IN THE BLOOD OF THE LAMB!
SATAN HAS <u>NOT</u> HAD THIS PRIVILEGE
AND NEVER WILL!